Timeshare Sales for the 21st Century

Timeshare Sales for the 21st Century

Andrew Arvedon and
Phil Symonds

2007

Timeshare Sales for the 21st Century

TABLE OF CONTENTS

INTRODUCTION

Timeshares have changed over the years, and so have consumers. With the advent of the internet cell phones, and other means of communication, they are more educated on the subject matter then they used to be. There are other timeshare books out there, and they are very good. **This** book is the most up to date and realistic portrayal of timeshare sales you can find.

We are still selling timeshares and have not been able to find extra training either online or in a book. We decided to put this training book together in the hopes of helping countless others in the timeshare industry. This information is not generalized by any means. The information you will find in this book is direct from our tables to you. In this book we will go over the basic fundamentals that a new salesperson and even a seasoned veteran may or will encounter during their professional career.

We want to be ***absolutely, positvley, clear!! After reading this*** _**book, you will not go out and sell every single person you meet. (But pretty damn close!)**_

What you learn in this book is not an exact science; it's a form of art. We will be giving you the tools and items you will need to hone your skills and your craft. Do not expect instant gratification after reading this book. The timeshare salesman never stops learning. Once you have mastered the examples and situations we have given you, only then will your painting be a masterpiece.

The professional time share salesman understands the law of averages, and they have learned to bend that law to their own personal will. "Some will, some won't, so what," is the understanding that you can't get every single customer.

The ones you do sell will take care of you and your family financially. More importantly, you will have changed **their** lives for the better by enhancing the quality time they now can spend.

Before we move on, we want to introduce ourselves to give you readers and idea of whom we are, what we are about, and how well we have done in the industry.

Andrew Arvedon: I started working when I was fourteen, my first job being at Arby's Restaurant. While working at Arby's I used to hang out at the mall nearby from my house and volunteer at a store called Funcoland. For those of you who don't know, Funcoland is now Electronics Boutique or Gamestop. The manager of the store liked me well enough and thought I would have enough potential that he broke the rules of the company and was able to hire me at the age of fifteen. Normally you had to be sixteen to work for the company. I worked at Funcoland part time, and proceeded to beat out full time employees and managers, not only in my store, but in the entire district in categories such as sales volume, average price per sale, and the number of commissioned items sold for a span of three months straight.

After working for Funcoland, I went onto working for Waldenbooks, and again led the district in number of club signups and sales volume for my duration with the company. Towards the end of my college days, I worked for a company called Marketstar which worked with such companies as Verizon and Sony to sell their products in retail stores. I was part of the Verizon project, and it was my job to stand inside of Best Buy and sell internet services to the customers that came into the store. For the four months I worked for them I was number 1 and 2 in sales volume, number of sales for the month in the entire New England Region.

I chose to leave Marketstar and pursue a career selling timeshares. I have worked for a resort in the North East area with my friend Phillip Symonds over the past five months (Feb 07-Current). I have made bonus three out of the five months that I have been there, coming in first one of those months in closing percentage, and third in sales volume.

When I first started in this industry, I thought I would do well, as I had done really well in the sales industry up until this point. Timeshare sales are by far the hardest sales industry a salesman can be in. It is however the most rewarding. Do not ever doubt yourself. I knew I had the talent to sell, but my first month in the industry I was not getting the results I thought I would. Always ASK FOR HELP!!! In this industry you can never stop learning. Once you have stopped learning, your going to find yourself out of the industry because you will get complacent. By asking for help, and by seeking out additional training wherever I could find it, I have risen to half of my potential. I can be a superstar in this industry, because I believe in myself. To get to my full potential I need to learn every day, and come into work every day ready to do battle. In this next section we will show you how to prepare yourself for work every day.

Phillip Symonds: I've been in the timeshare industry for over five years now, and I have loved every minute of it. It's just like going into battle except for the fact that it's a psychological battle, not a physical one. I enjoy the fact that I have honed my skills to the point where I can get anyone sitting in front of me, to agree with my point of view by transferring my thought into theirs. The end result is a lot of money. Not only have I been in timeshare sales, I've also been in the United States Army for fifteen years. I enjoy a challenge, and timeshares definitely has been very challenging at times. Just like any other challenge, it's been very rewarding also. I was a non-commissioned officer for several years in the army and held several leadership positions.

My biggest hope through writing this book is to supply every timeshare salesman with more of the imperative information that they have had a hard time finding. I understand how they feel, I felt the same way, but what I found was, if I had to keep relying on the internet, or other forms of media for that information I wouldn't get it. I understood that I was not the only one

searching for training in this specific field. As we know, leaders take the initiative, and I decided to help write this book so that this information could be provided. It is with my pleasure that I bring you all of the knowledge and experience I have obtained right to you. This information is valuable, I am not just any timeshare salesman, and I am a million dollar writer. I hope this book and my experience will prove to be as valuable to you as it has been for me.

PREPERATION

What we are going to show you many times throughout this book is how to be prepared, not only physically but mentally as well. A plan if you will. People do not plan to fail, they fail to plan. Before you go to work, make sure you're ready to go to work. There are several ways to accomplish this on a daily basis. This is absolutely necessary to have continued success in your timeshare career. You need to remember that if you are not prepared while going into work that could prove to be fatal. The tours you will encounter always will be prepared to see you.

- **YOUR VEHICLE**—is a reflection of you. If you are working in a location that requires you to drive your tour in your vehicle make sure the appearance of said vehicle is professional and clean. It's their perception of you that could mean a lot of money for you or no money at all.

- **YOU'RE APPEARANCE**—-each location has its own dress code, but in our experience most resorts prefer the guys to wear shirts, ties, slacks, and shiny shoes. When wearing this attire, make sure it's ironed and clean. This may sound elementary for you men, but with our experience you'd be very surprised of the appearances of some of the "salesman" that come to work. For you ladies out there, the same applies; always follow your companies dress policy and use common sense.

- **STATE OF MIND**—-leave the cares of home at home where they belong. You can't afford to think about outside things while at work, you will have enough things to think about at work without the trials and tribulations of home life.
  Tours can pick up your body language, just like you can pick up theirs. If they sense that something is amiss, then that psychological barrier between you and them (the wall) will not break. The same can be said for when you go home. Leave work at work, and home at home. One of the best ways to consistently have a clear state of mind is to do the very thing you're selling. TAKE A VACATION! While on your tables it will show through your body language and your demeanor and mannerisms that you are what you're selling.

- **FIRST IMPRESSIONS**——when picking up your tour no matter what horrific event happened during your last tour, no matter what has happened at work that day, suck it up and drive on. You can't go into a new tour negatively; your tour can pick up on this. If they feel your negativity, they in turn will become negative, which defeats the whole purpose of picking them up in the first place. You are shooting yourself right in the foot. It's hard enough selling a tour, try selling one that's already negative when you first

meet them because you have "negged" them out.
If you give everyone the same show, you will never
have to worry about negging yourself out. A wise
man once said…."fake it till you make it." Even if you
don't feel positive, and you had a bad experience
with your last tour, don't let it show. Remember your
job is more an art, then a science, so act as if you are
acting on a stage when you have too.

- **<u>PRODUCT KNOWLEDGE</u>**—-is probably one
of the most important things you can learn as a
salesman. If you don't know what you're selling, you
won't sell your product. You are the professional,
not the person sitting across the table from you.
You have to know more then them, or seem like you
know more then them. You need to research your
company and your craft till your head will explode
with info. Things you have to know about your
company entails; how long they have been around,
what their maintenance fees are, how often they go
up, and make damn sure you know everything there
is to know about the area that your resort resides in,
and other locations that are within driving distance
of the resort you work at. Most timeshare owners
will use their week and exchange with one of the
exchange companies that are affiliated with your
resort. In the event that your owner wishes to use
their week at the home resort(the resort you work
at), knowing all about the area and surrounding
areas is extremely crucial. Later in this book, we will
expand more on this topic, as far as the amount of
info you disseminate to your client.

CHARACTER TRAITS

It takes a certain type of character to become and stay successful in this industry. Every successful timeshare salesman exhibits certain qualities and traits that are a must for what they do. If they do not have these traits engrained within them, through time, training, and hard work, they can obtain these traits.

<u>QUALITIES YOU SHOULD HAVE</u>:

- **<u>Leadership qualities</u>**—-leaders listen. If you notice during any presentation, the ones that are talking the most usually aren't the ones that are making the most. God gave you one mouth and two ears for a reason. Do the math. You should have your "pitch" perfected. Once you know your pitch and product, you always know where you're going to go with what you say. The key is to listen to what they have to say, because they won't realize they are giving you all the bullets you need to sell them. The more bullets you have, the better chance you have of hitting your target. If your tour states that they like swimming pools, golf courses and nightclubs, then you need to emphasize those features throughout your presentation. Not mentioning these aspects is just plain stupid.

- **SETTING GOALS**—-a goal is a dream with an end date. It is a vision that has become reality. You should never run out of goals, because then you become complacent. Once you become complacent, you'll find yourself fired. You won't be selling anymore, or as much as you used too. A wise man once said…"you're only as good as your last sale." You should be talking about the future sales you're going to make, not the ones you already have. Most timeshare salesmen sit around and talk about what they have done and they don't concentrate on what they need to do. If you find yourself in this category, you better change fast. Remember folks, the goal is to get as many deals as possible, so why walk away with one deal per day, when you can walk away with two or three.

EXAMPLE:

ANDY: My goal is to consistently have two goals a week, and then once I have achieved this, I want three deals a week etc…

PHIL: If I get one deal a week I'm happy.

Andy had multiple goals. He was achieving one goal and wanted more. He is always going to be sharp mentally whereas Phil might get complacent and not reach his potential. After his first deal, Phil really could care less if he sells or not. This is not an exact scenario; this example is to give you guys a rough idea of the consequences of not having set any goals in this industry. Remember the whole goal is to get as many deals as possible, the more deals you get, and the more money you make. The whole reason your in timeshare let's face it…. the money!!!

- **GREED**——-timeshare salesman need this trait. If you don't want to sell every tour you have, if you don't want every potential client you can obtain, if you don't want to make the most money you possibly can make, then go to Taco Bell or Sears. In this industry there is no ceiling on the amount of money you can make per year. I don't know about you, but I'm one greedy bastard. That's why we're so successful. You don't have to be a miser, that's not the type of greed we're talking about here. We are talking about good greed. The kind of greed that's going to get your bills paid, the kind of greed that's going to insure you're financially secure, the kind of greed that's going to allow you to help those who are close to you.

- **THE WILL TO LEARN**——change is a beautiful thing…if you can see it for what it really is. It's the ability to change one's position in life, whether it is for better or worse. You chose for the better, that's why you're reading this book. If you were not constantly feeding your brain with the information it needs to provide you with the ability to sell this awesome product, you are becoming complacent.

In this industry this is the biggest sin, because now you have fallen into a deadly trap. The good old fashioned "canned pitch". A canned pitch is a presentation that you use every single tour but never cater to who is sitting in front of you. It's something you've memorized and have learned how to repeat, but you're telling not selling. You're there to sell these people your product not tell them about it, by just telling them about your product you are not telling them what the product can do for them and they see no value. How many times have you heard this at the end of your presentation? "He/she did such a great job at least I know there is another way to vacation now." If you consistently get this response, you better fix this quick. We're not saying change your pitch in any way, you're pitch should be the same every time, however depending on who you have in front of you, is when you tweak it Once you have catered your pitch to every tour you have, you can start to continue on this path of timeshare higher learning and you will have no choice but to have continued success. Once you stop learning you will surely stop earning.

MEETING YOUR TOUR FOR THE FIRST TIME

Okay, so it's game time, you've just gotten called to go pick up your tour what are you going to do?

This is where the rubber meets the road. Always make the first impression the best impression, and I'm sure you've heard that's the "lasting impression." Thank god, that in our profession, we're so good at what we do, we can change that perception of that first impression no matter how bleak it is.

No matter how shitty your last tour was, no matter what happened on the way to work that morning, no matter what happens to you at work, when you are going to meet your tour for the first time, you have to give every single person the same opportunity and same performance if not better then the last.

NEVER EVER EVER EVER EVER EVER EVER EVER EVER EVER EVER EVER EVER EVER EVER EVER EVER EVER EVER PREJUDGE SOMEONE!!!!!!!

At this point, this should be the first time you have ever seen these people. God forbid you happen to be hanging out in the guest reception area, like all the other unprofessional salesman "negging" themselves out, thinking they know who's going to buy and who's not. If they had that talent, the company would have paid them millions to weed out the tours that were not going to buy. Don't be one of those people!! Always go above and beyond. Remember the key is to give everyone the best show of your life. If you have a single guy so what?

That guy could have inherited money from a dead aunt. If you have a person wearing sweat pants and a sweatshirt, or look like they are neighbors with Oscar the Grouch, you never know. Likewise, don't think you have a deal in the bag if you're with a doctor, lawyer or someone that looks rich. How do you know what rich looks like? You don't!! So don't try!!

We're not going to lie to you. We have "negged" ourselves many times. When we actually sold some of the people we sold, we couldn't' believe it. Our mouths mentally dropped, and that is why we firmly believe never to prejudge.

On the flip side, how would you feel if someone prejudged you? Just because you had crappy clothes, were fat, hideous, smelled or looked like you jumped off the pages of **GQ. Everyone's money smells the same! MM-MM- GOOD.**

Here are some examples from our personal experiences.

<u>PHIL</u>: I remember this woman very well. She was short, fat, and disgusting. She had long, straight, greasy hair, and barley had any teeth in her mouth. Her clothes weren't very well maintained. To add insult to injury she brought about six of her children with her and they were all about my age and they were a spitting image of their mother. I was PISSED! I knew the next 90 minutes I was going to be wasting air.

I mean gee; I could have had the couple right before her, well groomed, nice smile. DAMN. Well it turns out; at the table talking to this woman she was already an owner of timeshare. She actually owned a few weeks. Amazingly they all happened to be very expensive weeks. At the end of my presentation, we were shaking hands and I felt like a part of the family. Even though in the back of my mind, I reminded myself to wash my hands. Not only did she purchase from me. She paid the whole thing off. For your rookies…that's called cashing out. I could not believe what I was seeing, and what I was involved in. What I defiantly learned was, I would never pre-judge again.

ANDY: It was late during the week, and I had not sold anything up until this point. I was next to go out and it was pouring outside, and I really just wanted to get the hell out of there. I'm all set to go home, when a late tour comes right through the door screaming about how it took him 3 hours to get to our resort, when it only should have taken him about an hour.

The guy was middle aged, single, balding, had glasses, wore Pee-wee Herman type pants and had a thick N.Y. accent. I said to myself are you fucking kidding me? It's fucking raining outside, I'm 0-4 for the week, I need to get a deal, and I'm stuck with this single piece of shit that is only here for his fucking gift.

I grudgingly went up to the counter to get the sign-in paperwork, and find out that the guy is retired, and only making about 40 grand a year. I said O.K. let's just get this over with. I sat the guy down, and he was extremely cold with me, because he was still mad about driving in the pouring rain all that time.

To make a long story short, at the end of the presentation, one of my mangers comes over and shows the guy the prices. The guy grabs the sheet and carefully looks over everything. He then points to the most expensive price and asks is this the down payment? My manager says yup. Even my manager gave me a look before he sat down to talk to the guy. Almost as if to say, are you fucking kidding me?? I have to talk to this guy? I'm wasting my turn on this guy??

The guy then pulls out around 7 different credit cards, and whips out his cell phone. Me and my manager both look at each other like ARE YOU KIDDING ME? THIS GUY IS GONNA BUY?

Even my sales director has his mouth hanging open. Remember guys, it was pouring its around 6 at night, everyone is waiting to go home, and this guy is calling every single credit card to find what the lowest interest rate would be to put down his deposit.

Long story short, the guy bought my product. Why? Because even though the guy sucked, and even though it was pouring out, I said to myself, what else am I going to be doing right now? I might as well give this guy the best show he's ever seen. Sure enough, the guy bought me.

That is why I will make an attempt never to pre-judge again. I'm still human, and from time to time the thought of prejudging will enter my mind, but I remember the Pee-wee Herman looking guy and that thought instantly gets squashed.

PHIL: I had a Resort director once who told all us salesman a story about Ewell Brenner. Ewell Brenner was the main actor for the play King and I on Broadway. At the end of each performance reporters would ask him how he thought he did, and he would always reply with that was the best performance of my life.

Make sure every one of your presentations if the best presentation of your career.

The moral to remember is never "neg" yourself out, if you do, you will not succeed.

Before you take your tours to your office or table, you need to greet them properly.

ANDY: First ask yourself how you would like someone to meet you and greet you. Would you want someone taking one look at you and assuming that you were broke, stupid, ugly, not worth the time, or would you want someone coming up to you and treating you like you just cured cancer?

PHIL: This is how you should greet someone every single time. First be very enthusiastic. Enthusiasm is very contagious. I don't know about you, but I don't think anyone has ever bought of a boring person. Look at the last four letters in the word enthusiasm. They are IASM....??? I AM SOLD MYSELF!!!!!!

If you're sold yourself, act like it, nothing can be worse then trying to sell a product you don't believe in.

This is a perfect greet...short and sweet...The reason you want to keep your greeting as short as possible is because you have no idea what has been said in the waiting area. Other tours might have become negative, in which case the people around them will become negative. You might find owners who are unhappy for some reason, complaining in the waiting area, and now your tour has to listen to that. Do you think someone is going to buy something when people like themselves are unhappy with the product? By getting them out of there as soon as possible, you are pulling them out of what could have been a negative environment, and through the power of association using your enthusiasm you have removed them from a negative environment into a positive one. Here is an example of a short meet and greet. "Mr. and Mrs. Jenkins...Mr. and Mrs. Jenkins...Hello my name is Phillip Symonds I'm going to be your personal representative today, please follow me to my office."

On the way to the office or sales pit which ever applies to you, is where you'll warm up to them and learn about who your sitting with. Always ask them on the way to your office or table (so how many timeshare presentations have you been on?) always assume that they have been on some.

This question will usually throw them off track because they are not expecting it. Their answer is usually truthful. Never ask them "have you ever been on a timeshare presentation before" because buyers are liars. You don't want to give them the opportunity to lie to you right up front. If they see the opportunity they'll take it. As a professional timeshare salesman you should always be in control.

ANDY: In the event that they say they still haven't been on a presentation before, but you have a feeling they are lying, say something to the effect of, "oh wow, I really wish you had, you would have saved me about 70 min on this presentation." When they realize that they won't have to be there 70 min they all of a sudden conveniently will remember the ones they have been on.

PHIL: If they have been on a presentation before, you need to ask them "oh great you own one right?" They most likely will say no. When they do, this is your opportunity to find out why. If we get all of the objections they had on the previous one out in the open, and beginning of your tour it will be easier to weed through the B.S. and overcome the objections before they come up in your presentation.

EXAMPLE:

PHIL: Oh you don't own? What was it that stopped you from purchasing from the last place you were at?

ANDY: They didn't have outdoor pools.

PHIL: Oh, so if they did have outdoor pools you would have joined that day?

ANDY: Well...no.

PHIL: Oh, so that wasn't the reason you didn't join. What was it?

ANDY: There was a lot of noise.

PHIL: Oh, so if there wasn't that much noise down there, you would have joined?

ANDY: No…

PHIL: Well then what was the real reason or number of reasons that stopped you from becoming an owner that day?

Keep on asking these questions until you come to the main reason. No matter what reasons they give you, most of the time it's the money. In reality 99 percent of the time, it's the money. If we gave them a program like this for free, no matter what resort it was at, they would take it in a second. By asking them these questions you are whittling it down to that topic. You are inherently letting them know that it is just the money. The reasons you hear that they didn't join, is still your duty to cover all of those objections in your presentation, so they don't come up at the end.

TABLE TIME

You've gotten them to your table, now it's time for your presentation. In this section we will show you the different types of people you may encounter, what to do and what not to do in certain situations, and how to stay in control of your table at all times.

There are certain types of people that you are going to encounter on your tables. What we will do for you guys is we will name these types of people and explain what they do and how to gain control of your table back.

"**THE STROKER**"—-no its not a character in a comic book, it's an actual type of person who will lead you to believe that you have a deal just to get out of the presentation in as little as time possible. The problem is that this type of person is doing everything you want them to do on a tour and saying everything you want to hear because you are not selling you are telling. The key is to get them involved in the presentation.

EXAMPLE:

PHIL: Steve and Kim do owning your vacations make sense to you?

THEM: UH HUH.

PHIL: Good, so you see the value?

THEM: UH HUH.

PHIL: Ok, great let's move on to this next part.

WRONG WRONG DANGER WARNING!!!!

Here is how it should be done.

ANDY: Steve and Kim, does owning your vacations make more sense then renting?

THEM: UH HUH

ANDY: I'm sorry guys what does uh huh mean?

THEM: Yes.

ANDY: Ok, great let's move on.

PHIL: You have to get them involved in your presentation. They have to be thinking about what you are actually saying. By sitting there and saying uh huh, uh huh, they are not thinking about what you are saying. The goal is to transfer your thought into their mind. The only way to do this is to get them to answer your questions with as many clear answers as possible.

"**THE EXPERT**"—-they seem to know everything about the product, they either don't or they are wrong.

EXAMPLE:

ANDY: Does this make sense?

THEM: Yes, I know this already, can we just hurry up?

ANDY: Sure, no problem it seems like you guys understand.

NO NO NO NO NO NO WRONG WRONG WRONG!!

PHIL: What Andy did was the wrong way to handle the situation. They want to get out of here as quickly as possible, and want Andy to cut corners. Andy thinks that these people might buy because they know everything and he does not want them to get angry because he is asking questions that to them seem stupid. In the process he is losing control of the table.

PHIL: Does this make sense?

THEM: Yes, can you hurry up, we already know this.

PHIL: Oh great. Here is my pen and paper, I've had a really long day, I've met with so many people, can you just hurry up and tell me what my program consists of since you already know all about it?
OR

PHIL: Oh great. Seeing as you already know about the benefits of our program, let's just skip to the end. How many weeks would you like to buy?

THEM: Ummm....

PHIL: This is usually the point where they start choking. I haven't lost control of my table. Always remember that they usually only are there for the gifts. They just want the gifts, and they will do anything to throw you off. They usually give you their best shot right up front. When you recognize this, smile because you know you have them right where you want them. They are using all their bullets in one shot, and they are afraid because you might sell them.

"**THE BIG SHOT**"—I have the money (or at least you would think so)

If you have a survey where you work, chances are when you ask this person where they vacation, they will respond with I have vacation homes everywhere, I don't need your program, I stay with friends all over the place, they love when I stay because I buy them dinners, my brother owns hotels in Vegas I stay for free etc....

Never forget what you are giving these people at the end. You are giving them gifts. Sit back and think a minute .If this person really owns vacation homes everywhere, and can vacation for free, and say their friends love when they stay.... why are they meeting with you? Do they really need a free vacation, when they already are staying for free? Obviously a person with lots of money, realizes that time=money, so why would they be wasting 90 min of their time?

"**THE NOT TODAY PERSON**"——As soon as you pick these people up for your tour, you will be hit with I'm not doing anything today. They will even tell you it's a policy they have never to do anything on the same day.

There are many ways to easily respond to this. You can do it the cute way, or you can do it the way that has worked for many salesmen.

CUTE WAYS:

"What day would be good for you?"

"How are you going to be able to choose your gifts today?"

"How are you even talking to me right now? You had to choose whether or not to come here today correct?"

"Ok, let's think this through. You never make decisions on the same day. You decided to wake up today right? You decided to get in your car to drive here correct? You decided to take this presentation correct? You decided to spend money on gas to get here correct? You decided to spend money on food so you can eat something either on the way here or on the way home? So with all due respect you can make decisions both mentally and financially on the same day cant you?"

"That's ok; I'll just show you what you would have had today."

The way I would recommend combating this person, is by saying the following: "That's ok, I'll treat you the same as everyone else."

Buyers are liars. Disregard everything they say. They are just throwing you off the scent. They may be sick maniacal people who determine whether or not they will buy from you depending on how you respond to them.

If you do this correctly you will never buy what they have to sell you. There is a deal on every table, you selling them, or them selling you. What determines a successful timeshare salesman is how often you get sold yourself.

SELLING VS TELLING

In the timeshare industry or any sales industry for that matter, there is a huge trap that every sales person at one time or another has fallen into. That trap is getting into the bad habit of just repeating what the product is, not what the product can do.

There is a difference between telling someone the apple is tasty, but not why the apple is tasty. You should learn how to sell the sizzle, not just the steak. You also have to create a problem and then solve it.

EXAMPLE:

ANDY: Guys, how nice would it be to go to Cancun for $199 dollars and stay in a 2 bedroom 2 bathroom Jacuzzi tub condo for a week? You would also have a kitchen, living room, and other amenities.

PHIL: Guys, how nice would it be to go to Cancun for $199 and stay in a 2 bedroom 2 bathroom Jacuzzi tub condo for a week, instead of staying in a cramped hotel room for $100 a night. Wouldn't it be nice to wake up in the morning and have a cup of coffee without having to get dressed, having to drive around early in the morning in an unfamiliar community? Wouldn't it be nice for the sheer convenience of grabbing a cup of coffee in your own kitchen?

Which example to you sounds like telling, and which sounds like selling?

Andy mentioned to the tour that they would be staying in a 2 bedroom condo with a kitchen, and other amenities but without anything to compare it to. There is no problem. The tour shrugs it off. They are not excited.

Phil shows them the difference in what they are doing now, and what they could be doing, and puts them in the picture of actually doing it. When you do this it stirs up the emotions of actually being in a 2 bedroom condo with the full amenities, and gets them to want what you have to sell them, because they want to have those same feelings all the time.

The difference between selling and telling is the difference in what your paycheck is and what it could be.

PHIL: I was taught at one point in my career, by a V.P. of the company that I was working for to tell and then show, not show and then tell. What he meant by this was, when you show someone your product no matter what aspect of the product it was, and then you tell them about it, your telling them something they already know, and it doesn't leave any room to build trust between you and your tour.

When you tell and show, you continuously back up what you have been telling them and you tend to build rapport and trust with your client to such a point when you ask them for their business they will have no choice but to say yes.

EXAMPLE:

PHIL: Mrs. Jenkins, here at our resort it could easily cost you as a non-owner 3-4 hundred dollars a night in peak season. (TELL) If you look right here at our rates for the general public it says 3-4 hundred a night. (Show)

The biggest thing to remember is to put them in the picture. What we are selling is abstract. They cannot touch it unless they use it. When they drive home as a new owner they can't look in their rear-view mirror and see the condo follow them. They have to rely on the mental pictures that we shared with them and helped them create. All they have is their paperwork and a handshake. Remember our job is more of an art than a science, so learn how to paint beautiful pictures in their minds and you will become successful at what you do.

BUILDING RAPPORT

A wise man once said. "You have to earn the right to sell them." What he meant by that, is you can't just ram information down these people's throats. When you first meet your people get to know them by warming them up. Ask where they are from, what they like to do, what they do for work etc…This is the process that warms them up and builds rapport. **NEVER BE THEIR FRIEND!!!**

<u>IF YOU WANT A FRIEND BUY A DOG</u>

Well your probably wondering to yourself, how can you talk with them and ask questions, but not sound fake at the same time? You have to care, but just not that much.
<u>EXAMPLE</u>:

<u>ANDY</u>: So what do you guys do for work?

<u>THEM</u>: I do graphic design.

ANDY: That's great I have a lot of friends who do graphic design.

OR

That's great, my brother does graphic design.

Another way to break those barriers down, is the "me too" method.

THEM: I love water skiing.

PHIL: ME TOO!

Use common sense. If they say they are a raging alcoholic, use your own judgment. As for myself, I'm going to say me too. Build rapport with them. Any common grounds you find while talking with them and share with them helps bring down the invisible barrier. During the presentation if you become their friend, it will be easier for them to say no at the end. There is a difference between empathy and sympathy.

Empathy means that you understand how they feel, but still carry on with your belief.

Sympathy means that you understand how they feel, and get off track and feel sorry therefore not giving 100 percent in your presentation.

EXAMPLE:

Sympathy:

THEM: This is really great, I like it, but I lost my job and I don't know what I'm going to do

ANDY: Oh I'm so sorry to hear that. Wow, that's a shame. Oh man, you know I really hope you find one, I feel bad for you guys. If you can't do this today I understand.

ARE YOU KIDDING ME????? WRONG WRONG WRONG

Andy sympathized with the person, but look what happened. It's easy to do, and you might know someone who has been in the same situation, but this is your job. Your not a counselor, your not their friend, you may feel bad, but you still need to support yourself, and your family. If you want a friend buy a dog.

Empathy:

THEM: This is really great, I like it, but I lost my job and I don't know what I'm going to do.

PHIL: I know how you feel, I felt the same way when I lost my job, but you know what I found?

WAIT FOR THEM TO RESPOND!!!!!!!

THEM: What?

PHIL: I found a job. Now let me ask you something. You're gonna find a job aren't you? Your not gonna go the rest of your life never working again right?

WAIT FOR THEM TO RESPOND

THEM: Yes.

PHIL: So that's exactly why you need to do this today. So when life hits you the hardest, or the next time you don't have a job, you know you can get away and have a guaranteed vacation the rest of your life. Money and life in general, can no longer stop you from getting what you deserve. You found time to come up here today, when you could have been looking for a job, so you couldn't be that worried about it right?

Phil understood how that person felt, but it did not faze him, he did not stray from his ultimate goal of giving 110 percent on his presentation. In situations when they are looking for sympathy for not doing something, the professional only gives empathy. One of the best ways to cover any objection is the "feel, felt found" method.I understand how you feel, others or I have felt that way, but what other or I have found is…..

BAG OF TRICKS

Having a bag of tricks is something that every timeshare salesmen should have, but you should only use it when needed. A lot of new timeshare salesmen, even some veterans tell all they know, when they should really know all they tell. When you throw every single piece of information at a tour, they get confused, their brain stops functioning and they lose any interest or any enthusiasm they had. This should not be a college lecture. This should be fun you're selling vacations!

KISS…. Keep It Simple Stupid.

Timeshare in general is simple. The concept is simple. You have a week, if you don't want to go to your home resort during that time; you can trade it go anywhere in the world at anytime. That's it.

Depending on where you are working, each resort will have special incentives, or programs designed for the consumer. Do not tell everything you know about timeshare to these people. Only tell what they ask. Only tell what pertains to the conversation at hand.

If you confuse these people too much, or you drone on and on like this book, you will bore them. If you send people home confused and disgruntled, chances are they will cancel. Your bag of tricks is like a golf bag. You pull out the clubs that you need to use for the hole that you're on. If you need to talk about trading power, pull it out, if you don't need to talk about it, why bring it up?

KEEPING CONTROL OF YOUR TABLE

The one thing you always need to remember while on your table is that your table is YOUR table. You should always have control of your table. Never let the tour run the show. They will try this using many different methods. In this section we will go over the different types of methods used by the tours we have faced in our careers. Sometimes the tours will do is purposely, other times by accident, but in either case, you need to address the situations when they come up at once.

STAR GAZING: Do you ever notice your tour looking up at the ceiling? We've always wanted to know what is so interesting up there too. That's why when our tours start to "star gaze" we stop what we are doing, and star gaze with them. The more the merrier!! Once you do this enough times, they will finally get the picture. When you mirror their behavior, you don't have to verbally tell them to stop; they will realize it and stop automatically. This is one of the best ways to stop them from taking control of the table. In the event that they do not stop, is when you should stop your presentation.
"What's so cool up there? I want to look too!"

You can also just non-verbally look up there with them, when you see that they have stopped what they are doing out of the corner of your eye, and then continue on with your presentation. To minimize this from continuing, you have to engage them with questions to keep their attention. If they happen to look at other people, do the same thing. Or you could ask…

ANDY: "Oh, wow…do you know those people?

THEM: "No."

ANDY: "Oh, because you keep on staring over there, is everything ok?"

THEM: "Um…yes…"

ANDY: "Ok. Good, let's continue on with this presentation and leave them alone."

THE LIAR: (BUYERS ARE LIARS)

PHIL: The best way that I can explain this type of person is through a story. This is an example of what I recently went through during a tour. Every single time I would ask my tour a question he would give me an answer. When I would reiterate his answer through an example, he would change his answer to the exact opposite of what he had said before.

If you ask a tour a question, and they answer it one way, and during the presentation they change their answer, you need to stop what you are doing, and handle the situation at hand.

EXAMPLE:

PHIL: If you could go anywhere in the world, what three places would you like to visit?

THEM: Paris, Italy, Houston.
LATER IN THE PRESENTATION:

PHIL: So, Jim, when you go to Italy through this exchange company on your dream vacation….

THEM: That's not my dream vacation; I have no interest going there.

PHIL: Whoa….Wait a minute…You told me on the survey your dream vacation was Italy. Are you being less then honest with me?
I
THEM: Uh..Oh…Um…No…But…I told you…

PHIL: Listen, every single time, you tell me one thing, and then I find out later on it's really another, we're going to be here a lot longer then both of us want to be here, so please give me honest answers and we can both get through this.

At this point, they realize that you are actually listening to everything they are saying, and you are remembering all of their answers, you are more professional than any other timeshare salesmen they have met, and nothing will get by you. This will make it harder for them to continue to lie to you because not only are you listening, you are confronting them on anything they have said that doesn't go along with what they have been telling you up till this point.

WHAT TO ASK PEOPLE WHO OWN TIMSHARE

Occasionally on your tours you will have people who already own timeshare. There are two different types of people who own timeshare who go to another timeshare presentation. The people who want another timeshare and the people who have a timeshare but are here for the gifts

You have to be careful in how you talk to each person. Think for a second. If they own a timeshare why are they here? Chances are the timeshare they have is not working for them. If it was, why on earth would they be wasting 90 more minutes to go to another timeshare presentation? You should automatically congratulate them on their purchase. Make them feel like they were the smartest people on the face of the planet. Play up what they have done. It will only help you in the end.

Questions you should ask them:

1. How long ago did you buy?
2. Where did you buy?
3. How big is the unit?
4. What week do you own? Is it points?

5.   How much are the maintenance fees?
6.   How many weeks do you own?
7.   What type of program do you have? An every year program, every other year tri-year?
8.   Is it a deed or a lease?
9.   Is it working for you?

If they say yeah its working great, then say great, then you obviously must be looking for another one, because why on earth would you be here right now, when you could on be vacation using your timeshare?

WAIT FOR THEIR RESPOSNE!!!!

If they balk, then say oh ok, well then let me show you how to use yours, and that's what we'll do. When they see that your willing to help them instead of sell them, you will have instant rapport, but all the while you will be finding faults in their program, you will be showing them why yours is more appealing.

OBJECTIONS

Here we are people. The section you've been waiting for; how to cover objections. We have compiled a list of major objections that we have overcome as salesman. We want you to realize that you will fail more then you will succeed. There are no magic words or sayings that will get people to do what you want. These are just answers to the most common smoke screens tours will throw at you. They can be easily overcome.

I'm buying a house.

PHIL: I understand how you feel; a lot of people have felt that way, what they have found is that they were in a better situation then most people. Did you know you can actually tie this into your mortgage? How smart would you be? Now you get a home that comes with a lifetime of vacations. The cost of this deed over 30 years only brings your payment up like 5 bucks a month. Congratulations all I need is your driver license and how you want to handle the down payment.

I have a car payment. (Or other payments)

ANDY: I understand how you feel, a lot of people have felt that way, but what they have found was, that even though they have these payments they were still going on vacation anyway. With all due respect we are not talking about your car money, your house money, your diaper money; we are talking about the money you spend on vacations anyway. With all due respect you told me earlier you had gone on numerous vacations before. So are you being less then honest with me? Ok, great, how would you like to handle the down payment?

I can't afford two timeshares.

PHIL: I understand how you feel, a lot of people have felt that way, but what they have found is that's exactly why they need to do this today. If you can't afford two timeshares now, what makes you think you can afford two timeshares later at tomorrow's price? You told me, that you wanted to give this to your two children. Listen folks, you wouldn't give your children one box with a sweater in it at Christmas and have them both fight over it would you? What do you think they are both going to do with one timeshare? What you need to do is rent the other one out or gift it to friends and family and remember that gift does not have to be a free gift.

I need to think about it.

ANDY: I understand how you feel, a lot of people have felt that way, but what they have found is they really don't need to think about it. It's pretty easy. You have two choices when you leave this table. You can continue renting hotel rooms at inflation rising prices, or you can choose to own your vacations while staying in beautiful places around the world for the same money. What would you choose to do?

ANDY: I understand how you feel, a lot of people have felt that way, but what they have found is wher. presented with the today offer which is only today, and the anytime offer which can be done after today, they realized that the best opportunity they were being presented was today. So by going home and thinking about it, they would not be able to take advantage of the today offer? Would you ever pay more to get less when you can pay less to get more?

ANDY: I understand how you feel, a lot of people have felt that way, but what they have found is by saying they need to think about it, they may not have all the answers or information they need. Is this the case? If so, please ask any questions you are unsure about.

Timeshare isn't for me.

ANDY: I understand how you feel, a lot of people have felt that way, but when they found that they could save money while going on great vacations they knew timeshare was for them.

ANDY: Ok. What's for you?

I have to talk to my financial advisor or accountant or lawyer.

PHIL: I understand how you feel, a lot of people have felt the same way, what they found is the last time they took a vacation they didn't ask their financial advisor. The same thing applies here today. We are only talking about vacations. When your financial advisor went on his vacation did he ask your help?

PHIL: What do you think your financial advisor would say? Do you think he'd say no to saving money and having great vacations? If so, then it's time with all due respect to find another financial advisor.

PHIL: That's great. You know what the attorney general means? The attorney general is the highest attorney in each state. Our company is governed by the laws that he sets. Do you think your lawyer would ever say no to something his boss has already said yes to? Of course not, let me show you how easy it is to get involved today.

We need to pray on it.

PHIL: (For those that believe in Jesus) Great! You believe in the word of God. The word of God says that he wants you to have the desires of your heart. He also says that when two come in his name and ask in Jesus' name it is done. So let's pray right now and believe and we shall receive. (Put your hands out, like you are going to pray with them, and wait for a response.) If they pray with you, you got a deal. They are not going against the word of God. If they don't, they've pretty much showed you they don't believe the Bible as the word of God. God as we know only rewards faith.

I can't make any decisions at all.

ANDY: You have already decided to go on vacation. I am showing you a choice. You either want to save money or you don't. Smart people save money. You're smart right?

I can't make any decisions without my boyfriend/ girlfriend/partner.

ANDY: That's great. How long have you been going out with said person. Great! Do you trust him? Do you trust her? Great! You must have money that is only yours right? Of course! So you and only you are the master of your money. You love this program and that's why you alone will join.

ANDY: Great. Is your boyfriend/girlfriend/partner a smart savvy consumer? I'm sure that's the case. Do you really think your partner would be proud of you if you spent money instead of saved money?

CLOSING

We hope this book will help you get started in your new exciting career. There is tons more to be learned every day in this industry. Once you stop learning, you stop earning. By purchasing this e-book you have taken the correct step in bettering not only your career, but yourself and your way of life. Always remember you must fail often to succeed only once.

Quitters never win and winners never quit. Remember in this industry if you persist long enough and your consistent long enough you win. You have to remember you will not sell everyone. A wise man once said. Out of every ten people there are two you will sell, there are two you won't, and the remaining six is where you are judged.

Someone is always sold on every table. Was it you?

VISIT TIMESHAREDUDES.COM TO DOWNLOAD OUR AUDIO FILES THAT GO WITH THE EBOOK.

FOR CONTINUED SUCESSES AND UP TO DATE INFO, SIGN UP FOR OUR NEWSLETTER WHICH GIVES

YOU ALL THE CURRENT INFORMATION ON HOW TO BATTLE YOUR TOURS ON THE TABLES. MORE OBJETIONS, MORE CHARACTER TRAITS, MORE TYPES OF TOURS, MORE CONDITIONS, AND 1 ON 1 HELP. TIMESHAREDUDES.COM WE'LL SEE YOU THERE!